contents

D0480605

Number & Algebra

Shape, Space & Measurement   19 - 30

Handling Data   31 - 33

Top row: 100 1 2 3 4 5 6 7 8 9 10 11 12 13 14 15 16 17 18 19 20 21 22 23 24 25

Right column: 26 27 28 29 30 31 32 33 34 35 36 37 38 39 40 41 42 43 44 45 46 47 48 49

Bottom row: 75 74 73 72 71 70 69 68 67 66 65 64 63 62 61 60 59 58 57 56 55 54 53 52 51 50

Left column: 99 98 97 96 95 94 93 92 91 90 89 88 87 86 85 84 83 82 81 80 79 78 77 76

ODD NUMBERS

1 3 5
7 9 11 13
15 17 etc.

2 will NOT go exactly into ODD numbers

EVEN NUMBERS

2 4 6
8 10 12 14
16 18 etc.

All numbers that 2 will go into EXACTLY are EVEN numbers

MULTIPLES

Every number has MULTIPLES. e.g. every number that 3 will go into is a MULTIPLE of 3. 3, 6, 9, 12, 15, 18 ....etc. are all multiples of 3.

FACTORS

Every number has FACTORS. The FACTORS of 12 are 1, 2, 3, 4, 6 and 12 because all of these numbers go exactly into 12. 1 is a FACTOR of every number but it is NOT a Prime number.

PRIME NUMBERS

2, 3, 5, 7, 11, 13, 17 ... etc. PRIME NUMBERS have only 2 factors, themselves and 1.

PRIME FACTORS

PRIME FACTORS are FACTORS which are also PRIME NUMBERS. e.g. 2 and 3 are PRIME FACTORS of 12.

SIGNS and WORDS used in MATHEMATICS

 Addition (add), plus, sum, total. $4 + 3 = 7$

Subtraction (subtract), minus, take-away. $7 - 3 = 4$

Multiplication (multiply), times, product. $3 \times 5 = 15$

Division (divide), sharing. $15 \div 5 = 3$

---

is **Equal to** (the same value). $\frac{1}{2} = 0.5$

is **Not Equal to** (different value). $3 \neq 4$

 or is **Approximately Equal to** $\frac{1}{3} \approx 0.3$

is **Equivalent to** $5^2 \equiv 5 \times 5$

 Therefore   **Because**

 Parallel to $\perp$ **Perpendicular** (at 90° to).

Less than ($x < 3$, reads x is less than 3).

Greater than ($x > 5$, reads x is greater than 5).

Less than or Equal to ($y \leqslant 4$, reads y is less than or equal to 4).

Greater than or Equal to ($y \geqslant 7$, reads y is greater than or equal to 7).

TIMES TABLES 1-6

There are not as many to learn as you think.

ONE

1 x 1 = **1**
2 x 1 = 2
3 x 1 = 3
4 x 1 = 4
5 x 1 = 5
6 x 1 = 6
7 x 1 = 7
8 x 1 = 8
9 x 1 = 9
10 x 1 = 10
11 x 1 = 11
12 x 1 = 12

TWO

1 x 2 = 2
2 x 2 = **4**
3 x 2 = 6
4 x 2 = 8
5 x 2 = 10
6 x 2 = 12
7 x 2 = 14
8 x 2 = 16
9 x 2 = 18
10 x 2 = 20
11 x 2 = 22
12 x 2 = 24

THREE

1 x 3 = 3
2 x 3 = 6
3 x 3 = **9**
4 x 3 = 12
5 x 3 = 15
6 x 3 = 18
7 x 3 = 21
8 x 3 = 24
9 x 3 = 27
10 x 3 = 30
11 x 3 = 33
12 x 3 = 36

FOUR

1 x 4 = 4
2 x 4 = 8
3 x 4 = 12
4 x 4 = **16**
5 x 4 = 20
6 x 4 = 24
7 x 4 = 28
8 x 4 = 32
9 x 4 = 36
10 x 4 = 40
11 x 4 = 44
12 x 4 = 48

FIVE

1 x 5 = 5
2 x 5 = 10
3 x 5 = 15
4 x 5 = 20
5 x 5 = **25**
6 x 5 = 30
7 x 5 = 35
8 x 5 = 40
9 x 5 = 45
10 x 5 = 50
11 x 5 = 55
12 x 5 = 60

SIX

1 x 6 = 6
2 x 6 = 12
3 x 6 = 18
4 x 6 = 24
5 x 6 = 30
6 x 6 = **36**
7 x 6 = 42
8 x 6 = 48
9 x 6 = 54
10 x 6 = 60
11 x 6 = 66
12 x 6 = 72

The numbers in yellow are the ones you've already learnt. If you look closely they have appeared in a previous table.

The numbers in boxes are called square numbers - why? $4 \times 4 = 16$

visit www.daydreameducation.co.uk for more information

TIMES TABLES 7-12

There are not as many to learn as you think.

SEVEN

1 x 7 = 7
2 x 7 = 14
3 x 7 = 21
4 x 7 = 28
5 x 7 = 35
6 x 7 = 42
7 x 7 = **49**
8 x 7 = 56
9 x 7 = 63
10 x 7 = 70
11 x 7 = 77
12 x 7 = 84

EIGHT

1 x 8 = 8
2 x 8 = 16
3 x 8 = 24
4 x 8 = 32
5 x 8 = 40
6 x 8 = 48
7 x 8 = 56
8 x 8 = **64**
9 x 8 = 72
10 x 8 = 80
11 x 8 = 88
12 x 8 = 96

NINE

1 x 9 = 9
2 x 9 = 18
3 x 9 = 27
4 x 9 = 36
5 x 9 = 45
6 x 9 = 54
7 x 9 = 63
8 x 9 = 72
9 x 9 = **81**
10 x 9 = 90
11 x 9 = 99
12 x 9 = 108

TEN

1 x 10 = 10
2 x 10 = 20
3 x 10 = 30
4 x 10 = 40
5 x 10 = 50
6 x 10 = 60
7 x 10 = 70
8 x 10 = 80
9 x 10 = 90
10 x 10 = **100**
11 x 10 = 110
12 x 10 = 120

ELEVEN

1 x 11 = 11
2 x 11 = 22
3 x 11 = 33
4 x 11 = 44
5 x 11 = 55
6 x 11 = 66
7 x 11 = 77
8 x 11 = 88
9 x 11 = 99
10 x 11 = 110
11 x 11 = **121**
12 x 11 = 132

TWELVE

1 x 12 = 12
2 x 12 = 24
3 x 12 = 36
4 x 12 = 48
5 x 12 = 60
6 x 12 = 72
7 x 12 = 84
8 x 12 = 96
9 x 12 = 108
10 x 12 = 120
11 x 12 = 132
12 x 12 = **144**

The numbers in yellow are the ones you've already learnt.
If you look closely they have appeared in a previous table.

The numbers in boxes are called square numbers - why? 8 *8 x 8 = 64*

KNOW YOUR NUMBERS
INTRODUCING NUMBERS 1 TO 10

I'm ONE. I'm ODD but I'm not prime.
I'm made up of 1 x 1. (only one factor 1)

I'm TWO. I'm EVEN, the only even PRIME.
I'm made up of 2 x 1. (two factors 2 and 1)

I'm THREE. I'm ODD and PRIME.
I'm made up of 3 x 1. (two factors 3 and 1)

I'm FOUR. I'm EVEN but I'm not prime.
I'm made up of 4 x 1 and 2 x 2. (three factors 4, 2 and 1)

I'm FIVE. I'm ODD and PRIME.
I'm made up of 5 x 1. (two factors 5 and 1)

I'm SIX. I'm EVEN but I'm not prime.
I'm made up of 6 x 1 and 3 x 2. (four factors 6, 3, 2 and 1)

I'm SEVEN. I'm ODD and PRIME.
I'm made up of 7 x 1. (two factors 7 and 1)

I'm EIGHT. I'm EVEN but I'm not prime.
I'm made up of 8 x 1 and 4 x 2. (four factors 8, 4, 2 and 1)

I'm NINE. I'm ODD but I'm not prime.
I'm made up of 9 x 1 and 3 x 3. (three factors 9, 3 and 1)

I'm TEN. I'm EVEN but I'm not prime.
I'm made up of 10 x 1 and 5 x 2. (four factors 10, 5, 2 and 1)

*Notice the PRIME NUMBERS 2, 3, 5, and 7
have only two factors, themselves and 1*

FIGURES ARE FUN

PATTERNS

Look for the patterns in numbers, for example, the nine-times table.

These numbers go from 0 to 9			These numbers go from 9 to 0
1 x 9 =	**09**		0 + 9 = 9
2 x 9 =	**18**		1 + 8 = 9
3 x 9 =	**27**		2 + 7 = 9
4 x 9 =	**36**		3 + 6 = 9
5 x 9 =	**45**		4 + 5 = 9
6 x 9 =	**54**		5 + 4 = 9
7 x 9 =	**63**		6 + 3 = 9
8 x 9 =	**72**		7 + 2 = 9
9 x 9 =	**81**		8 + 1 = 9
10 x 9 =	**90**		9 + 0 = 9

Each answer adds up to 9.
The answers for 1 to 5 are the reverse of the answers for 6 to 10:

5 x 9 = 45	4 x 9 = 36
6 x 9 = 54	7 x 9 = 63

CAN YOU SPOT PATTERNS IN OTHER TABLES?

MAGIC SQUARES

All the columns (↑) rows (→) and diagonals (✕) add up to the same number.

8	**3**	**4**	= ?
1	**5**	**9**	= ?
6	**7**	**2**	= ?
= ?	= ?	= ?	

What do they add up to ?
Can you make your own magic square ?

SQUARE NUMBERS

These numbers are called square numbers. Can you see why?

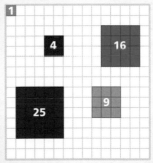

1 x 1 =	1
2 x 2 =	4
3 x 3 =	9
4 x 4 =	16
5 x 5 =	25

1, 4, 9, 16, 25, ...
This is called a sequence, which is a list of numbers in a pattern. Can you continue the sequence?

TRIANGLE NUMBERS

These numbers are called triangle numbers. Can you see why?

•	**1**	add 2 more
(balls)	**3**	add 3 more
(balls)	**6**	add 4 more
(balls)	**10**	add 5 more
(balls)	**15**	and so on ...

There is a sequence with these numbers:
1, 3, 6, 10, 15, ...
Can you draw more balls and continue the sequence?

MULTIPLICATION CHART

✕	1	2	3	4	5	6	7	8	9	10	
1	1	2	3	4	5	6	7	8	9	10	1
2	2	4	6	8	10	12	14	16	18	20	2
3	3	6	9	12	15	18	21	**24**	27	30	3
4	4	8	12	16	20	24	28	32	36	40	4
5	5	10	15	20	25	30	35	40	45	50	5
6	6	12	18	24	30	36	42	48	54	60	6
7	7	14	21	28	35	42	49	56	63	70	7
8	8	16	**24**	32	40	48	56	64	72	80	8
9	9	18	27	36	45	54	63	72	81	90	9
10	10	20	30	40	50	60	70	80	90	100	10
	1	2	3	4	5	6	7	8	9	10	✕

SPOT THE PATTERNS

*The **ORANGE** numbers are all square numbers.*
Notice that 3 × 8 = 24 and 8 × 3 = 24
*Can you spot any other patterns? The figures in **GREEN**
give you a clue but there are many more.*

visit www.daydreameducation.co.uk for more information

PRIME NUMBERS

A **prime number** is a whole number that has only two **factors**: itself and 1.
For example, **7** is a prime number because it has only two **factors**.

$$7 \div 7 = 1$$ and $$7 \div 1 = 7$$

1	2	3	4	5	6	7	8	9	10
11	12	13	14	15	16	17	18	19	20
21	22	23	24	25	26	27	28	29	30
31	32	33	34	35	36	37	38	39	40
41	42	43	44	45	46	47	48	49	50
51	52	53	54	55	56	57	58	59	60
61	62	63	64	65	66	67	68	69	70
71	72	73	74	75	76	77	78	79	80
81	82	83	84	85	86	87	88	89	90
91	92	93	94	95	96	97	98	99	100

PRIME - MATES

13 is a prime number.
It has two factors.
$13 \div 1 = 13$ $13 \div 13 = 1$

2 is the lowest and only
even prime number.
It has two factors.
$2 \div 1 = 2$ $2 \div 2 = 1$

1 is not a prime number.
It has only one factor.
$1 \div 1 = 1$

6 is not a prime number
It has four factors:
1, 2, 3 and 6.
$6 \div 1 = 6$ $6 \div 2 = 3$
$6 \div 3 = 2$ $6 \div 6 = 1$

EQUIVALENCE

May look different but has the same meaning, power or value.

SUM ≡ AMOUNT ≡ TOTAL

These words look different but they all have the same meaning.

One Pound (£) ≡ **One Pound (£)** ≡ **One Pound (£)**

These 3 sets of coins look different but all have the same spending power.

$$\frac{1}{2} \equiv \frac{2}{4} \equiv \frac{4}{8}$$

These 3 fractions look different but all have the same value (equivalent fractions).

Equivalent fractions are found by multiplying or dividing the TOP and the BOTTOM by the SAME NUMBER.

a) by multiplying

$$\frac{2^{\times 2}}{3_{\times 2}} \equiv \frac{4}{6}$$

b) by dividing

$$\frac{15^{\div 5}}{20_{\div 5}} \equiv \frac{3}{4}$$

this is called cancelling down

Fractions are only equivalent when you multiply or divide
the **TOP** and the **BOTTOM** by the **SAME NUMBER**.

FRACTIONS DECIMALS PERCENTAGES

| FRACTION | → DIVIDE NUMERATOR BY DENOMINATOR → | DECIMAL | → MULTIPLY BY 100 → | PERCENTAGE |

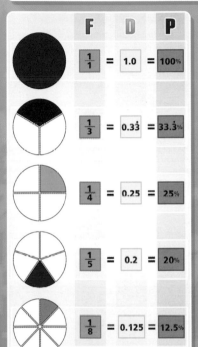

	F		**D**		**P**
⬤	$\frac{1}{1}$	=	1.0	=	100%
◑	$\frac{1}{3}$	=	0.33$\dot{}$	=	33.$\dot{3}$%
◴	$\frac{1}{4}$	=	0.25	=	25%
◔	$\frac{1}{5}$	=	0.2	=	20%
❋	$\frac{1}{8}$	=	0.125	=	12.5%

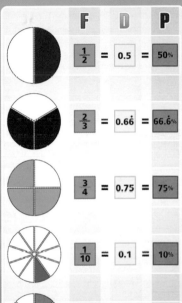

	F		**D**		**P**
◐	$\frac{1}{2}$	=	0.5	=	50%
◕	$\frac{2}{3}$	=	0.66$\dot{}$	=	66.$\dot{6}$%
◔	$\frac{3}{4}$	=	0.75	=	75%
❋	$\frac{1}{10}$	=	0.1	=	10%
❋	$\frac{3}{8}$	=	0.375	=	37.5%

| FRACTION | ◁ *CONVERT TO FRACTION | DECIMAL | ◁ DIVIDE BY 100 | PERCENTAGE |

* WHEN CONVERTING DECIMALS TO FRACTIONS FIND THE DENOMINATOR AND THEN CANCEL DOWN IF NECESSARY:-

0.1	=	ONE TENTH	=	$\frac{1}{10}$		0.5	=	$\frac{5}{10}$	=	$\frac{1}{2}$
0.01	=	ONE HUNDREDTH	=	$\frac{1}{100}$		0.25	=	$\frac{25}{100}$	=	$\frac{1}{4}$
0.001	=	ONE THOUSANDTH	=	$\frac{1}{1000}$		0.125	=	$\frac{125}{1000}$	=	$\frac{1}{8}$

REMEMBER: " PER CENT" MEANS " OUT OF 100"   "OF" MEANS "MULTIPLY"

daydream EDUCATION

www.daydreameducation.co.uk

SIMPLE FRACTIONS

A **'fraction'** is part of a whole.
When Tommy **'fractured'** his leg, a **whole** bone had broken into **two pieces**.

A number fraction is when one unit is split into an equal number of pieces.
This fraction is called a half :

*This is called the **numerator**.*
It shows how many of that type of fraction.

*This is called the **denominator**.*
It shows the type of fraction.

$$\frac{1}{2}$$

Each of the three shapes has been split into 2 equal pieces. Each piece is called one half.
One half ($\frac{1}{2}$) is pink and one half ($\frac{1}{2}$) is white.

This fraction is called three quarters (or three fourths) :

Numerator: *3 of the 4 pieces.*

$$\frac{3}{4}$$

$\frac{1}{4}$	$\frac{1}{4}$
$\frac{1}{4}$	$\frac{1}{4}$

Denominator: *4 equal pieces.*

Each shape has been split into 4 equal pieces. Each piece is called one quarter (fourth).
Three quarters ($\frac{3}{4}$) are yellow and one quarter ($\frac{1}{4}$) is white.

Fraction wall showing some equivalent fractions.

| $\frac{1}{12}$ | $\frac{1}{12}$ | $\frac{1}{12}$ | $\frac{1}{12}$ | $\frac{1}{12}$ | $\frac{1}{12}$ | $\frac{1}{12}$ | $\frac{1}{12}$ | $\frac{1}{12}$ | $\frac{1}{12}$ | $\frac{1}{12}$ | $\frac{1}{12}$ |

| $\frac{1}{6}$ | $\frac{1}{6}$ | $\frac{1}{6}$ | $\frac{1}{6}$ | $\frac{1}{6}$ | $\frac{1}{6}$ |

| $\frac{1}{3}$ | $\frac{1}{3}$ | $\frac{1}{3}$ |

| $\frac{1}{8}$ | $\frac{1}{8}$ | $\frac{1}{8}$ | $\frac{1}{8}$ | $\frac{1}{8}$ | $\frac{1}{8}$ | $\frac{1}{8}$ | $\frac{1}{8}$ |

| $\frac{1}{4}$ | $\frac{1}{4}$ | $\frac{1}{4}$ | $\frac{1}{4}$ |

| $\frac{1}{2}$ | $\frac{1}{2}$ |

| **1** |

SIMPLE PERCENTAGES

The word *'percent'* comes from two Latin words *'per'* and *'cent'* meaning *'out of every 100'*.

The symbol for percent is %.

In percentages, the whole amount equals 100%.

So 20% means 20 out of 100.

British History 1800 to 1900

A CENTURY is 100 years.

TO FIND A PERCENTAGE OF AN AMOUNT

 CONVERTING TO A FRACTION

To find 20% of £40:

 Convert the percentage to a fraction by writing the percentage over 100.

$$20\% = \frac{20}{100}$$

Multiply the fraction by the amount.

$$\frac{20}{100} \times 40 = \frac{800}{100}$$

Convert the improper fraction to a whole number.

$$800 \div 100 = 8$$
20% of £40 = £8

 FINDING 10%

To find 20% of £40:

Calculate 10% of £40.

10% of 40 =
40 ÷ 10 = 4

 Multiply 4 by 2 to get 20%.

4 × 2 = 8
20% of £40 = £8

TO EXPRESS ONE QUANTITY AS A PERCENTAGE OF ANOTHER

Percentages are used to express how large or small one quantity is relative to another quantity. For example, percentages are often used to express test scores.

Beth scored 30 out of 50 on her maths test. What percentage is her score?

1 Divide Beth's score by the total number of questions.

30 ÷ 50 = 0.6

2 Multiply this by 100 and add a percentage sign.

0.6 × 100 = 60%

Beth scored 60% on her maths test.
We can check this by using equivalent fractions:

$$\frac{30}{50} = \frac{60}{100} = 60\%$$

daydream

RATIO

Ratio is a way of comparing two or more quantities.

Purple paint is made by mixing blue and red paint in a ratio of 2 to 3.

Blue
2 litres

Red
3 litres

Purple
5 litres
(2:3)

The ratio can be written in the following formats:

| 2 to 3 | 2:3 | 2/3 |

2   **1**

In pastry dough, the ratio of flour to butter is 2:1.

5   **2**

In mortar, the ratio of sand to cement is 5:2.

2   **6**   **3**

The money is split between Lilly, Jack and John at a ratio of 2:6:3.

A ratio must be written in the correct order, with the quantity mentioned first written first.

The ratio of boys to girls is 3:4.

NOT

The ratio of boys to girls is 4:3.

Note that the ratio of girls to boys is 4:3.

ALGEBRA

The word **algebra** comes from the Arabic words **'Al Jabr'** meaning **'the reunion of broken parts'**.

In **algebra** we use letters to help us, as well as numbers and the ordinary signs of arithmetic (**+ − × ÷**).

Algebra is like a game you can play.

Think of a number - don't tell me!

Think of a number. Let's call it 'n'.

3

Double it.

Double it.
2 x n or 2n

$2 \times 3 = 6$

Add four.

Add four.
2n + 4

$6 + 4 = 10$

What's your answer?

What's your answer?
10

Ten

So **2n + 4 = 10**

You thought of **3**

In **algebra** this is called an **equation**.
Solving this equation means finding the value of 'n'.
For Sally to find 'n' she takes 4 from 10 and divides by 2.

In other words she works backwards

$10 - 4 = 6, \quad 6 \div 2 = 3.$ **n = 3**

Algebra is like all games, it has rules. If you learn the rules, you can play the game.

GRAPHS AND CO-ORDINATES

**A GRAPH HAS FOUR DIFFERENT QUADRANTS
WHERE THE x AND y CO-ORDINATES ARE EITHER POSITIVE OR NEGATIVE**

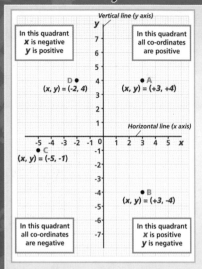

Vertical line (y axis)

In this quadrant
x is negative
y is positive

In this quadrant
all co-ordinates
are positive

D •
$(x, y) = (-2, 4)$

• A
$(x, y) = (+3, +4)$

Horizontal line (x axis)

• C
$(x, y) = (-5, -1)$

• B
$(x, y) = (+3, -4)$

In this quadrant
all co-ordinates
are negative

In this quadrant
x is positive
y is negative

**When plotting points
the ORDER is VITAL
THINK of the ALPHABET
x before y**

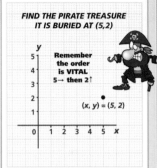

**FIND THE PIRATE TREASURE
IT IS BURIED AT (5,2)**

Remember
the order
is VITAL
5→ then 2↑

$(x, y) = (5, 2)$

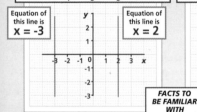

Vertical lines passing through the X axis

Equation of
this line is
$x = -3$

Equation of
this line is
$x = 2$

Horizontal lines passing through the Y axis

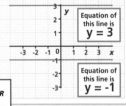

Equation of
this line is
$y = 3$

Equation of
this line is
$y = -1$

**FACTS TO
BE FAMILIAR
WITH**

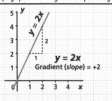

Lines sloping uphill left to right have a positive gradient

$y = 2x$
Gradient (*slope*) = +2

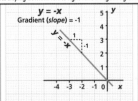

Lines sloping downhill left to right have a negative gradient

$y = -x$
Gradient (*slope*) = -1

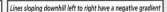

AREA AND PERIMETER

The perimeter is the total distance around the outer edge.
The area of a figure is the amount of space inside the perimeter.

SQUARE

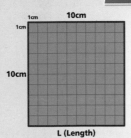

The **AREA** of the square is:
10 x 10 = 100 square cm (100cm²)

The **PERIMETER** of the square is:
10 + 10 + 10 + 10 = 40cm

In short: AREA = L x L = L²
PERIMETER = L + L + L + L = 4L

RECTANGLE

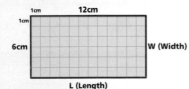

The **AREA** of the rectangle is:
6 x 12 = 72 square cm (72cm²)

The **PERIMETER** of the rectangle is:
6 + 12 + 6 + 12 = 36cm

In short: AREA = L x W and PERIMETER = L + W + L + W = 2L + 2W

OTHER SHAPES

When measuring more complex shapes, break them down into basic shapes.

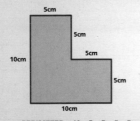

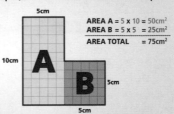

AREA A = 5 x 10 = 50cm²
AREA B = 5 x 5 = 25cm²

AREA TOTAL = 75cm²

PERIMETER = 10 + 5 + 5 + 5 + 5 + 10 = 40cm

daydream
TEL 0800 064 0122
www.daydreameducation.co.uk

ANGLE PROPERTIES

Take a triangle

Angles in a triangle add up to 180°

Tear off the angles

They add up to 180°

Angles on a straight line add up to 180°

Take a quadrilateral

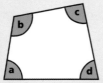

Angles in a quadrilateral add up to 360°

Tear off the angles

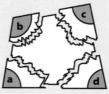

They add up to 360°

Angles around a point add up to 360°

ANGLE PROPERTIES OF PARALLEL LINES

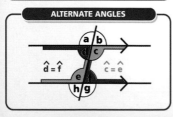

CORRESPONDING ANGLES

$\hat{a} = \hat{e}$ $\hat{b} = \hat{f}$

$\hat{d} = \hat{h}$ $\hat{c} = \hat{g}$

ALTERNATE ANGLES

$\hat{d} = \hat{f}$ $\hat{c} = \hat{e}$

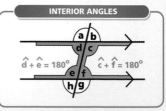

VERTICALLY OPPOSITE ANGLES

$\hat{a} = \hat{c}$ $\hat{b} = \hat{d}$

$\hat{e} = \hat{g}$ $\hat{f} = \hat{h}$

INTERIOR ANGLES

$\hat{d} + \hat{e} = 180°$ $\hat{c} + \hat{f} = 180°$

ANGLES
AND THEIR
MEASUREMENT

The turn or rotation between two meeting lines is called an angle and is measured in degrees. A protractor is used to measure angles.

There are 360° (degrees) in 1 complete rotation, 180° in half a rotation and 90° in a quarter rotation.

360°

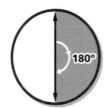

180°

90°

ACUTE ANGLES

Angles less than 90° are called **acute angles**.

45° 62° 75° 32°

RIGHT ANGLES

90° angles are called right angles and are marked with a small square.

90° 90° 90° 90° 90° 90°

OBTUSE ANGLES

Angles greater than 90° but less than 180° are called obtuse angles.

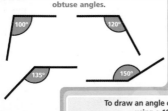

100° 120° 135° 150°

REFLEX ANGLES

Angles greater than 180° are called reflex angles.

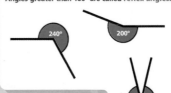

240° 200° 330°

To draw an angle of 200° (reflex angle) using a 180° protractor

Take the angle to be drawn from 360° e.g.   360° - 200° = 160°

Now, using your protractor, draw an angle of 160°

160°
200°

You have also drawn an angle of 200°

LINES

VERTICAL

Straight up and down.

HORIZONTAL

Flat and parallel with the ground.

DIAGONAL

Straight line corner to corner.

PARALLEL

Lines that never meet.

VERTEX

VERTEX →

Angle, corner, highest point.

PERPENDICULAR

At right angles (90°).

BISECT

To cut in half.

ARC

Part of the circumference of a circle.

GET IN SHAPE
AND KNOW THEIR NAMES

SQUARE

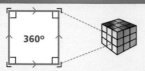

360°

- 4 sides of equal length
- 4 equal angles of 90°
- 4 corners (vertices)
- 2 pairs of parallel sides

RECTANGLE

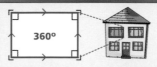

360°

- Opposite sides of equal length
- 4 equal angles of 90°
- 4 corners (vertices)
- 2 pairs of parallel sides

EQUILATERAL TRIANGLE

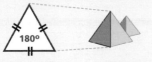

180°

- 3 sides of equal length
- 3 equal angles of 60°
- 3 corners (vertices)
- No parallel sides

CIRCLE

πr^2

Radius
Diameter
Circumference

- **Cirumference** - the outer edge of a circle.
- **Diameter** - the distance from one edge of a circle to another, passing through the centre.
- **Radius** - the distance from the centre of a circle to its edge.

REGULAR PENTAGON

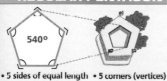

540°

- 5 sides of equal length
- 5 equal angles of 108°
- 5 corners (vertices)
- No parallel sides

REGULAR HEXAGON

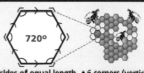

720°

- 6 sides of equal length
- 6 equal angles of 120°
- 6 corners (vertices)
- 3 pairs of parallel sides

REGULAR OCTOGON

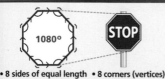

1080°

- 8 sides of equal length
- 8 equal angles of 135°
- 8 corners (vertices)
- 4 pairs of parallel sides

TRAPEZIUM

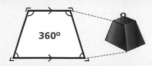

360°

- 4 sides of varying length (2 may be equal)
- 2 pairs of equal angles
- 4 corners (vertices)
- 1 pair of parallel sides

QUADRILATERALS

Quadrilaterals have 4 sides and 4 angles, the angles always add up to 360°.

SQUARE

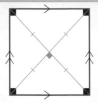

4 equal sides
4 equal right angles (90°)
Opposite sides are parallel
Diagonals are equal and bisect each other at 90°

RECTANGLE

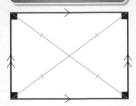

Opposite sides are equal
4 equal right angles (90°)
Opposite sides are parallel
Diagonals are equal and they bisect each other

RHOMBUS

4 equal sides
Opposite angles are equal
Opposite sides are parallel
Diagonals are not equal but bisect each other at 90°

PARALLELOGRAM

Opposite sides are equal
Opposite angles are equal
Opposite sides are parallel
Diagonals are not equal but bisect each other

TRAPEZIUM

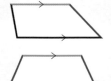

4 sides, two of which are parallel

KITE

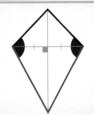

2 pairs of adjacent sides are equal
1 diagonal bisects the other at 90°
1 pair of opposite angles is equal

TYPES OF TRIANGLES

EQUILATERAL
(Equi - Equal, Lateral - Sides)

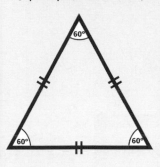

3 equal sides,
3 equal angles (each 60°)

ISOSCELES
(Greek - Two Equal Sides)

2 equal sides,
2 equal angles (base angles)

RIGHT ANGLE
(Right Angle - 90°)

One angle is a right angle (90°)
Two other angles add up to 90° (a + b = 90°)
The longest side is called the **HYPOTENUSE**

SCALENE
(Greek - Skelanos - Unequal)

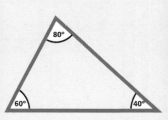

All angles are different,
all sides are different.

REMEMBER: IN ANY TRIANGLE THE 3 ANGLES ADD UP TO 180°

VOLUMES AND AREAS

PYRAMIDS AND CONES

Volume = $\frac{1}{3}$ × Base Area × Height

$(V = \frac{1}{3} \times A \times H)$

CONE

PYRAMID

SPHERES

Volume = $\frac{4}{3}$ × π × Radius³

$(V = \frac{4}{3}\pi r^3)$

SPHERE

AREAS

TRIANGLE

Area (A) = $\frac{1}{2}$ × b × h

TRAPEZIUM

Area (A) = $\frac{1}{2}(a + b) \times h$

PARALLELOGRAM

Area (A) = b × h

CIRCLE

Area (A) = πr^2

CUBES AND CUBOIDS

Volume = Length × Width × Height

$(V = L \times W \times H)$

CUBE

CUBOID

PRISMS

Volume = Cross Sectional Area × Length

$(V = A \times L)$

TRIANGULAR PRISM

CIRCULAR PRISM (CYLINDER)

SOLIDS AND THEIR NETS

A Solid Figure has flat surfaces (faces), edges, and corners (vertices).
A net is the surface of a solid shape folded out flat.

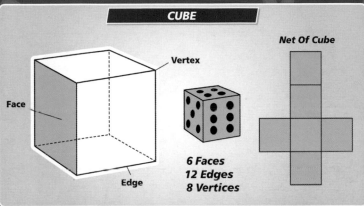

CUBE

Vertex

Face

Edge

Net Of Cube

6 Faces
12 Edges
8 Vertices

TRIANGULAR PRISM

5 Faces
9 Edges
6 Vertices

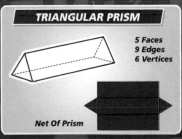

Net Of Prism

CUBOID

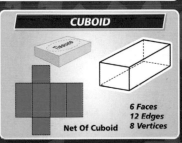

6 Faces
12 Edges
8 Vertices

Net Of Cuboid

SQUARE-BASED PYRAMID

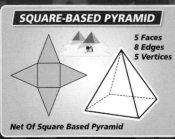

5 Faces
8 Edges
5 Vertices

Net Of Square Based Pyramid

TRIANGULAR-BASED PYRAMID (TETRAHEDRON)

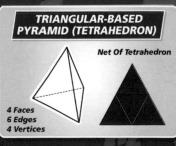

Net Of Tetrahedron

4 Faces
6 Edges
4 Vertices

The surface area of a solid figure is equal to the total area of its net.
Work out the areas of the separate parts of the net and add them all together.

daydream
education

TEL 0800 068 0232
www.daydreameducation.co.uk

SYMMETRY

A line of symmetry, also known as a line of reflection, divides an object into two parts that are the same size and shape.

A **square** has **4 lines** of symmetry.

An **equilateral triangle** has **3** lines of symmetry.

A **regular pentagon** has **5** lines of symmetry.

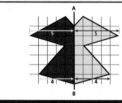

This shape has one line of symmetry. All corresponding parts are equidistant from the line of symmetry.

The butterfly offers an example of line symmetry that occurs in nature. It has one line of symmetry.

ROTATIONAL SYMMETRY

An object has rotational symmetry if it returns to its original form at any point when it is rotated around a central point.

The **square** has rotational symmetry of **order 4**.

The letter **H** has rotational symmetry of **order 2**.

The **recycling symbol** has rotational symmetry of **order 3**.

The **flower** has rotational symmetry of **order 6**.

It returns to its original form every **90° rotation**.

It returns to its original form every **180° rotation**.

It returns to its original form every **120° rotation**.

It returns to its original form every **60° rotation**.

The order of rotational symmetry of any regular polygon is the same as the number of lines of symmetry it has and the number of sides.

MEASUREMENT

LENGTH

Units used - Millimetre ___ ___tre (cm), Metre (m___

___ = 1 cm   100 ___   ___ 1000 m = 1 km

Hannah Jumps 2.25 m which is 225 cm and also 2250 mm

START
1 m
2 m
3 m

Christopher ran 1500 m
1500 m = 1.5 km

> REMEMBER - The word ' Kilo ' means 1000
> so 1 Kilometre = 1000 metres

WEIGHT / MASS

Units used - Gram (g), Kilogram (kg).

1000 g = 1 kg

This piece of cheese has a mass of 350 grams

WEIGHT IN GRAMS

The total mass of these apples is 1800 g which is 1 kg 800 g or 1.8 kg

This football weighs 500 g which is 0.5 kg or $\frac{1}{2}$ kg

> REMEMBER - The word ' Kilo ' means 1000
> so 1 Kilogram = 1000 grams

TIME

60 seconds = 1 minute
60 minutes = 1 hour
24 hours = 1 day

There are 12 hour clocks and 24 hour clocks.

12 HOUR CLOCK		24 HOUR CLOCK
12:00 Midnight	=	00:00
3:00 am	=	03:00
7:30 am	=	07:30
9:00 am	=	09:00
12:00 Midday	=	12:00
6:15 pm	=	18:15
11:00 pm	=	23:00

12 hours are a.m.
(Midnight to Midday)

12 hours are p.m.
(Midday to Midnight)

In a 24 hour clock there are 24 hours

CAPACITY

Units used - Litres (l), Millilitres (ml).

1 Litre = 1000 millilitres (ml)

Cola

1.5 litre

This cola bottle has a capacity of 1.5 litres which can be written as 1 litre 500 ml or as 1500 ml.

TIME

There are **60** seconds in each minute.

There are **60** minutes in each hour.

30 minutes after or **past** each hour
30 minutes before or **to** each hour

There are **24** hours in one day.

12 hours from midnight to midday (a.m.)
12 hours from midday to midnight (p.m.)

Remember		
60 seconds = 1 minute	60 minutes = 1 hour	24 hours = 1 day

Wake up! It's morning

7:15 a.m.
quarter past seven (a.m.)
15 minutes past 7 (a.m.)

Time for School

8:40 a.m.
twenty to nine (a.m.)
20 minutes to 9 (a.m.)

Yummy! Lunchtime

12:20 p.m.
twenty past twelve (p.m.)
20 minutes past 12 (p.m.)

Home time

3:30 p.m.
half past three (p.m.)
30 minutes past 3 (p.m.)

Dinnertime

5:45 p.m.
quarter to six (p.m.)
15 minutes to 6 (p.m.)

Sweet Dreams

9:00 p.m.
nine o'clock (p.m.)

daydream

AVERAGES

MEAN

The **MEAN** of a set of data is the sum of the values divided by the number of values.

$$\text{MEAN} = \frac{\text{SUM OF VALUES}}{\text{NUMBER OF VALUES}}$$

Joe was pleased with his exam results:

FRENCH	MATHS	ENGLISH	GEOGRAPHY	BIOLOGY	ART	MUSIC
79%	**81%**	**77%**	**88%**	**72%**	**88%**	**68%**

His **MEAN** mark was $\dfrac{79 + 81 + 77 + 88 + 72 + 88 + 68}{7} = \dfrac{553}{7} = $ **79%**

MODE

The **MODE** of a set of data is the value which occurs most often.

GEOGRAPHY **88%**

ART  **88%**

The **MODE** for Joe's results was 88%. It occurred twice, in Geography and Art.

MEDIAN

The **MEDIAN** is the middle value when the data is arranged in order of size.

MUSIC	BIOLOGY	ENGLISH	FRENCH	MATHS	GEOGRAPHY	ART
68%	**72%**	**77%**	**79%**	**81%**	**88%**	**88%**

The **MEDIAN** for Joe's results is 79% because the French result is in the middle.
If there is an even number of values, then the **MEDIAN** is the **MEAN** of the middle two.

PROBABILITY

Probability is used in everyday life to predict the chance of things happening.

Probability is measured on a scale of 0 to 1

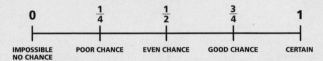

0	$\frac{1}{4}$	$\frac{1}{2}$	$\frac{3}{4}$	1
IMPOSSIBLE NO CHANCE	POOR CHANCE	EVEN CHANCE	GOOD CHANCE	CERTAIN

You must write probability as a FRACTION, DECIMAL OR PERCENTAGE

ESTIMATED PROBABILITY = $\dfrac{\text{NUMBER OF SUCCESSFUL EVENTS}}{\text{TOTAL NUMBER OF EVENTS}}$

The probability of scoring a *FOUR* when rolling a fair dice is

$P(4) = \dfrac{1}{6}$

The probability of scoring an *EVEN* number when rolling a fair dice is

$P(\text{EVEN NUMBER}) = \dfrac{3}{6}$

The probability of getting a *HEAD* when tossing a fair coin is

$P(\text{HEAD}) = \dfrac{1}{2}$

TREE DIAGRAMS

Using a tree diagram helps to solve probability problems involving combined events.

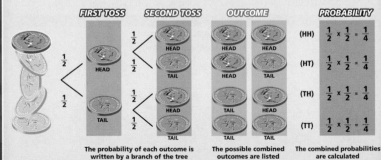

FIRST TOSS	SECOND TOSS	OUTCOME	PROBABILITY
		(HH)	$\frac{1}{2} \times \frac{1}{2} = \frac{1}{4}$
		(HT)	$\frac{1}{2} \times \frac{1}{2} = \frac{1}{4}$
		(TH)	$\frac{1}{2} \times \frac{1}{2} = \frac{1}{4}$
		(TT)	$\frac{1}{2} \times \frac{1}{2} = \frac{1}{4}$

The probability of each outcome is written by a branch of the tree

The possible combined outcomes are listed

The combined probabilities are calculated

When the outcome of one event does not affect the outcome of another, the events are independent.

DISPLAYING DATA

PICTOGRAMS

Pictograms show a picture or symbol to represent a number of people or items.

e.g. CD sales in a store = 1000.

SEPT = 3500

OCT = 3250

NOV  = 5000

DEC  = 6500

LINE GRAPHS

Line graphs are drawn by plotting points and then joining the points together with a line.

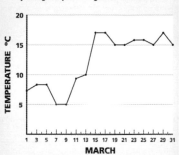

This line graph shows the midday temperatures in March.

BAR CHARTS

Bar charts can be used to display data that is grouped.

Abigail has a dog.

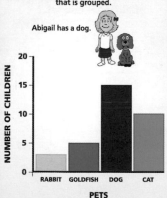

PIE CHARTS

This pie chart shows pupils' favourite sports.

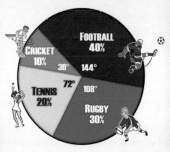

e.g. Rugby
30% of the pupils prefer rugby.
30% of 360° = 0.3 x 360°
= 108°

Like our Pocket Posters?

...then you'll love our award-winning A1 Wall Charts and Interactive Content Packs.

A1 Wall Charts

All of the posters contained in this book are available as A1 Wall Charts, from only £3.95.

Visit **www.daydreameducation.co.uk** to see our full range of Wall Charts.

Paper: from £3.95	Laminated: from £7.50

A1 (594mm x 840mm)

Interactive Content Packs

FROM ONLY £8 SITE LICENCE

See our Pocket Posters come to life with our award-winning Interactive Content Packs.

The Content Packs are ideal for use on whiteboards, projectors, individual PCs and Macs.

Approved by

Also available for your VLE (learning platform)

Visit **www.daydreameducation.co.uk** for more information and your **FREE** downloadable Content Packs worth up to £250!